Special thanks to our adviser:
Susan Kesselring, M.A., Literacy Educator
Rosemount–Apple Valley–Eagan (Minnesota) School District

# There Are
# Millions of
# Millionaires

MILLIONAIREVILLE
Population 8,000,000+

and other Freaky Facts About Earning, Saving, and Spending

by Barbara Seuling
illustrated by Ryan Haugen

PICTURE WINDOW BOOKS
Minneapolis, Minnesota

Editor: Christianne Jones
Designer: Abbey Fitzgerald
Page Production: Melissa Kes
Art Director: Nathan Gassman
The illustrations in this book were created digitally.

Picture Window Books
151 Good Counsel Drive
P.O. Box 669
Mankato, MN  56002-0669
877-845-8392
www.picturewindowbooks.com

Printed in the United States of America.

All books published by Picture Window Books
are manufactured with paper containing at least
10 percent post-consumer waste.

**Library of Congress Cataloging-in-Publication Data**
Seuling, Barbara.
There are millions of millionaires : and other freaky facts about
earning, saving, and spending / by Barbara Seuling ; illustrated
by Ryan Haugen.
p. cm. — (Freaky facts)
Includes index.
ISBN 978-1-4048-4115-4 (library binding)
ISBN 978-1-4048-4120-8 (paperback)
1. Finance—Juvenile literature. 2. Millionaires—Juvenile literature.
3. Money—Juvenile literature. I. Haugen, Ryan, 1972- ill. II. Title.
HG173.8.S48 2009
332.024—dc22                              2008006339

# Table of Contents

**Chapter 1**

And the Rich Get Richer:
Millionaires, Billionaires,
and Earnings........................... 4

**Chapter 2**

Securities and Insecurities:
Banks, Insurance, Credit,
and Saving................................ 12

**Chapter 3**

For What It's Worth:
Collectibles, Valuables,
and Spending............................ 20

**Chapter 4**

Bills, Wills, and Taxes.... 30

Glossary.......................... 36
Index.............................. 38
To Learn More................... 40

MILLIONAIREVILLE
Population 8,000,000+

And the Rich Get Richer:
Millionaires, Billionaires,
and Earnings

There are more than 8 million millionaires and more than 1,000 billionaires in the world.

In 1916, John D. Rockefeller became the first billionaire.

In medieval times, doctors sometimes covered pills in gold. This made the pills more acceptable to wealthy customers.

One of the most ruthless businessmen of all time was Marcus Licinus Crassus of ancient Rome. One of the services he provided was a fire brigade. This brigade rushed to burning buildings, then waited around until Crassus got paid before they would attempt to save it.

Millionaire Cornelius Vanderbilt of New York went into business for himself at the age of 16. He bought a small boat to bring people from Staten Island to Manhattan. Vanderbilt was worth $105 million when he died in 1877. He was worth more than the U.S. Treasury at that time.

Andrew Carnegie worked as a bobbin boy at a textile mill at the age of 13. He got paid $1.20 a week. Later, he sold his steel company for $480 million to J.P. Morgan.

In 1848, John Jacob Astor was the wealthiest man in the United States. He didn't believe in philanthropy. However, after he died, he left $400,000 in his will to establish a public library in New York City.

Philanthropist John D. Rockefeller made his first charitable contribution at the age of 16. By the time he died at the age of 97, he had given away about $550 million.

Rockefeller used to carry dimes around with him to give away. During the Great Depression, he switched from dimes to nickels.

Sarah Breedlove (Madame C.J. Walker) was born into slavery and orphaned by the age of 7. She worked hard to survive. Breedlove saw a need for a hair product and invented a hot comb that could manage thick hair. She did everything she could to sell her product. Her company kept growing. She became the first self-made female millionaire in the United States.

Hetty Howland Green, known as the richest woman of her time in 1916, left an estate estimated at around $100 million. The stories about her unwillingness to part with her money are legendary. One story claims her son went without medical treatment while she looked for a free clinic, resulting in the loss of his leg.

The first child to earn $1 million was young film star Shirley Temple. She had an estimated $1 million before she was 10 years old.

Daisy Alexander, heiress to the Singer sewing machine fortune, wrote out a will, stuck it in a bottle, and threw it into the River Thames in London. She died two years later. Ten years after her death, an unemployed restaurant worker, Jack Wurm, noticed a bottle in the sand as he walked along the beach. The paper said the finder of the message should receive half of Daisy's fortune, which amounted to about $6 million. The other half went to her lawyer.

John F. Kennedy was the wealthiest president the United States has ever had. On his 21st birthday, his father gave him a $1 million trust fund.

In his mid-20s, millionaire Jean Paul Getty retired for a few years after he made his first million dollars. It is said that Getty put a pay phone in his mansion after visitors kept running up large long-distance bills.

Walt Disney's first cartoon production company went bankrupt.

One of America's greatest fortunes, that of the Stern family, was built on birds. Max Stern started his business by selling singing canaries. The Sterns owned the Hartz Mountain Corporation, which specializes in pet foods and accessories, until 2000.

The Sultan of Brunei lives in a $400 million palace. It has 1,788 rooms, 257 toilets, five swimming pools, and much more.

The world's richest woman is Liliane Bettencourt of France. She is worth $20.7 billion. Her father founded L'Oréal cosmetics. Liliane inherited the company in 1957.

The richest American is Bill Gates. He is worth $53 billion. He is also the richest person in the world.

In 2006, professional golfer Tiger Woods became the first athlete in history to make $100 million in one year.

David Geffen dropped out of college and didn't have any career plans. He ended up co-founding Dreamworks film studios, which is worth more than $3 billion.

Robert McCulloch, who made his fortune as the creator of McCulloch's chain saws, bought London Bridge for $2,460,000. He then had it transported from its place across the River Thames in London, where it had stood for more than 100 years, to Arizona. This move cost him an additional $7 million. The bridge is the second most popular tourist attraction in Arizona (first is the Grand Canyon).

Author J.K. Rowling was a single parent with no money before the Harry Potter series was published. Now she is one of the wealthiest women in the world.

When Thomas Jefferson was president in the early 1800s, great wealth was considered to be $300,000. Today, you cannot make Forbes magazine's list of the richest Americans unless you have at least $1 billion.

One of the biggest bank mistakes of all time helped Melchor and Victoria Javier Jr. become millionaires. In 1977, the couple ordered a $1,000 bank draft from the Mellon Bank in Pittsburgh. The bank accidentally added three zeros to the draft, sending them $1 million. The bank tried to get the money back, but the Javiers refused to pay.

Records show that crime in the United States increases during periods of success. It declines during hard times.

## Securities and Insecurities:
Banks, Insurance, Credit, and Saving

There is evidence that Babylonian temples were depositories for money and places where loans were made.

Writing checks is not a modern idea. Checks were inscribed on clay tablets in ancient Babylonia and used as money.

In 1374, the first known modern check was written in Europe.

The first public bank in the world was in Barcelona, Spain. It opened in 1401.

The oldest surviving bank in the world is most likely the bank of Monte dei Paschi di Siena in Italy. It was founded in 1472. It has more than 1,800 branches around the world today.

In the 1500s, modern banks opened in Italy.

The word *bank* comes from the Italian word *banca*, which means "bench." Businessmen used to meet outside on benches to discuss money matters. These informal meetings would often end in loans or other investment deals.

In the early 14th century, bankers from northern Italy introduced money-lending to London. Several of England's kings were financed by their services.

The first loan taken out by the U.S. government was made on September 13, 1789. It was used to pay the salaries of the president and members of Congress. The money was borrowed from the Bank of North America.

The Bank of England once issued banknotes that were cut in half. This helped protect shipments of money to the branch offices. Each shipment contained only half of the money, so that highway robbers intercepting shipments would gain nothing.

There were no banks in the Colonies before the American Revolution. If you wanted to borrow money, you had to go to an individual for a loan.

In 1805, the Farmer's Bank of Annapolis, Maryland, was the first bank in the United States to pay interest on deposits.

American banks originally printed their own money called banknotes. With the thousands of different banknotes in circulation, people were very confused. To end the confusion, the U.S. government started printing one national currency in the 1860s. They also passed laws so banks could no longer print money.

The first recorded bank robbery in American history was in 1831. Edward Smith stole $245,000 from the City Bank on Wall Street in New York.

The great American comedian W.C. Fields did not like to carry cash. Instead, he opened a bank account wherever he was. He claimed to have 700 accounts around the world.

The piggy bank is not named after the pig. It is named after a kind of clay. Almost every home once had kitchen utensils made of a common clay known as pygg. Money was often kept in a household pot or jug made of this material. These containers came to be called pygg banks, or pyggy banks.

You are never too young to start a bank account. At the Young Americans Bank in Denver, Colorado, all of the customers are under the age of 22. The average customer is 9 years old and has a balance of about $480. Parents cannot make any changes to the child's account without the child's signature.

# Securities and Insecurities:
## Banks, Insurance, Credit, and Saving

Ove Nordström of Spånga, Sweden, has more than 5,750 different piggy banks. The collection started in 1957. It includes banks from more than 40 countries.

In ancient Rome, funerals were lavish affairs, much like weddings today. Citizens joined together to help pay the costs. They gathered money and wine, which was split among members of their families as necessary. It was an early form of life insurance.

The first life insurance policy came about in the mid-1500s. In a bar, some men convinced William Gybbons into paying them $80. If he died within the year, they would pay his widow $200. When William Gybbons died in a hit-and-run accident, the court upheld the contract.

The insurance on men's jewelry costs about twice as much as that on women's jewelry because men are found to be less careful about jewelry than women are.

Credit cards can be used to pay for just about anything, including bail. In Maryland, you can post bail and get out of jail with a credit card.

Cash is not the preferred source of payment in the United States. About 80 percent of all sales are paid for by check or credit card.

Walter Cavanagh of Santa Clara, California, has a record 1,497 credit cards.

# Securities and Insecurities:
# Banks, Insurance, Credit, and Saving

In the United States, there are about 125 million checking accounts.

The currency vault in Fort Knox, Kentucky, was built by the U.S. government in 1936 to hold gold bullion. It has an underground vault so secure that it cannot be penetrated even by an atomic blast.

The Federal Reserve Bank in New York City houses the world's largest store of gold. Every bit of gold that goes into the bank must be accounted for.

The first person to receive monthly Social Security payments was Ida M. Fuller of Ludlow, Vermont. She received check number 00-000-001 for $22.54 on January 31, 1940.

Worldwide, people in the United States save the least amount of money. On average, they save just 4.1 percent of their income. That's about four pennies for every dollar they take in.

## For What It's Worth:

Collectibles, Valuables, and Spending

In 1989, a man paid $4 for a framed painting at a garage sale. When he got home and took the painting out of the frame, he found a copy of the Declaration of Independence. In 1991, it sold at an auction for $2.4 million.

Button Gwinnett, one of the men who signed the Declaration of Independence, died in a duel a year after the signing. Only 30 known Gwinnett autographs exist. Today, his autograph is the most rare of all the Declaration signers. It is worth more than $100,000.

A book borrowed from the University of Cincinnati Medical Library in 1823 was returned in 1968 by the borrower's great-grandson. The fine was calculated at more than $20,000.

Dr. Seuss' original book, *To Think That I Saw It on Mulberry Street*, was rejected 27 times. A first edition copy of the book is now worth thousands of dollars.

Baseball cards started out as promotional gimmicks included in cigarette packs. But in 1931, gum companies thought of packing baseball cards with their penny packs of newly-invented bubble gum. What started as a hobby, collecting the cards is now a million-dollar industry.

From 1909 to 1911, a baseball card with the picture of Pittsburgh Pirates player Honus Wagner was placed in cigarette packages. Wagner, a nonsmoker, objected to having his picture appear in a promotion for cigarettes. The cards were withdrawn, but a few remained in circulation. Today, 24 cards still exist. In 2007, one of the cards sold for $2.35 million.

In 1993, an envelope bearing two 1847 Post Office Mauritius stamps sold for $3.8 million.

In 1918, a man named William T. Robey bought a sheet of 100 24-cent airmail stamps at a Washington, D.C., post office. When he discovered the airplane on the stamps had been printed upside down, he sold the stamps to a dealer for $15,000. A week later, the stamps were sold again for $20,000. Today, each of those 24-cent stamps is worth more than $200,000.

A 1963 G.I. Joe figure sold for $200,000 at an auction in Dallas, Texas, in 1993.

SALE!!
$200,000

The most expensive toy in the world is probably a dollhouse created by Neville Wilkinson. It took him 15 years to complete. The house contains 16 rooms and 2,000 miniature works of art. It was purchased for about $200,000 by the owners of "Legoland," a family theme park in Billund, Denmark. The dollhouse is on display there.

The most valuable comic book is Action Comics No. 1. It cost a dime when it first came out in 1938. Now it is worth about $350,000.

The FBI was once brought in to break up a ring of comic book forgers. A collector from Cambridge, Massachusetts, traded several expensive comic books for one rare one, only to suspect later that it was a fake. It turned out not to be fake after all but one of three different real versions of the book.

Gertrude Stein and her brother Leo were the only people who wanted Picasso's work when he was a young painter in Paris. Leo bought his first painting from Picasso for about $30. Picasso's paintings are now worth millions.

On May 15, 1990, Vincent Van Gogh's portrait of his physician, Doctor Paul Ferdinand Gachet, drew a record $82.5 million at an auction at Christy's in New York.

In 1908, the original Model T Ford cost about $850. In the 1920s, the price dropped to about $300.

Pens and Post-it notes are valuable office supplies. In fact, employees steal more than $50 billion a year in goods from their employers each year.

In 1896, it cost about 10 cents to get into the first movie theater in the United States. Today, it costs an average of $7.

In 1939, the average annual income in the United States was about $2,000. A television set cost around $500 then, which would have been about one-fourth of a year's income.

In 1988, a collector paid more than $7 million for a flawless 52.59-carat rectangular-cut white diamond.

In 2005, an early Ming Dynasty bowl sold for a world-record price of $3.9 million.

In 2004, Stuart Weitzman designed the world's most expensive pair of shoes. The "Cinderella" sandal is worth $2 million.

The most expensive condiment in the world is Ca Cuong, a secretion produced by beetles in Vietnam. It costs almost $100 for just 1 ounce (28 g).

The largest shopping mall in the world is in Canada. The mall is in Edmonton, Alberta, and has 800 stores.

The word *spend* comes from the Latin word *expendere*, which means "to weigh out."

Shells were once used to buy things. The most valuable shells were those of the cowrie, a sea snail with a colorful shell.

The coastal Indians of North America used shell money known as wampum.

Barley was the first acceptable form of money used in Mesopotamia.

Cattle were used as money in early Rome.

When knights returned home from crusades in medieval times, they counted beans among the most valuable treasures brought home from the East.

The Spanish conquerors of Mexico in the 16th century found the treasure houses of the Aztec Indians filled more with mountains of cacao beans than with gold or silver. The beans were prized for their food value and were used as currency throughout Central America.

# For What It's Worth: Collectibles, Valuables, and Spending

In 1574, the town of Leyden, Holland, was under siege. Money disappeared, along with household silver, as people hoarded their valuables. In order to have currency for everyday trade, the town took its books from the town library, tore out the pages, glued several together, and stamped them as if they were metal. After the siege, the "book money" was redeemed, and the town's library was started over again.

Dried codfish was used as money in Newfoundland in colonial days.

Gizzi pennies, long twisted rods of iron used as money by a tribe of West Africa, serve as money only while they remain unbroken. If they break, the "soul" is believed to have escaped. Only the tribe's high priest can fix a penny.

On an island called Yap in the South Pacific, the heaviest money in the world can be found. It is in the form of stone wheels. Some are as small as dinner plates, while others are 12 feet (3.7 m) across. The wheels are cut from limestone, quarried from an island 250 miles (400 km) away. They are brought back on rafts. Yap chiefs own the largest stones and stand them by their doorways to show off their wealth and importance.

# For What It's Worth: Collectibles, Valuables, and Spending

At one time, sugar was more valuable as money than as food in the West Indies.

Instead of coins or dollar bills, tobacco was once used as money in the southern United States.

Iron nails were used as small change in colonial times. Nails were so highly prized that a man might burn down his house to recover the nails.

On Santa Cruz Island, northeast of Australia, natives still use bird feathers to buy things from each other.

Hard-packed tea leaves, pressed into bricks, were used as currency in Tibet, Mongolia, and some parts of Siberia.

Other objects that have been used as money at different times around the world include the jawbones of pigs, coal, porpoise teeth, hard candy, fish bones, and the red scalps of woodpeckers.

## Time to Pay Up:
### Bills, Wills, and Taxes

In 17th-century Canada, money from France had not arrived in time to pay French soldiers stationed there. For temporary use, paper money had to be printed on playing cards.

The earliest document dealing with money was a "bill" inscribed in clay from ancient Babylonia, about 5,000 years old. It showed what a buyer owed to a merchant in exchange for goods.

In ancient Egypt, bread was used as currency. It even appears as payment on an ancient payroll. Pictures of royal bakeries were included in the fancy murals in the tombs of pharaohs to show their wealth.

George Washington's expenses for winning the American Revolutionary War came to about $160,074.

In 1833, Robert Owen, a Welsh social reformer, set up a plan in England to issue "labor notes." These were paper currency based on hours of a man's labor. The notes were in denominations of numbers of hours and were in existence for one year.

Americans spend four times as much money on pet food as they do on baby food.

The territory of Alaska was purchased from Russia in 1867 for only two cents an acre. The bill totaled just $7.2 million.

Francois Rabelais, the 16th-century writer, said in his will: "I have nothing; I owe a great deal; the rest I give to the poor."

In his will, William Shakespeare left his wife his second best bed. In those days, it was common for the best items to go to the children.

The longest will on record was that of Mrs. Frederick Cook, the American widow of a British drapery manufacturer. The will was 95,940 words long, bound in four volumes, explaining how she wanted her fortune of $100,000 distributed.

Czar Peter I of Russia ordered men to shave off their beards. Those who refused had to pay a fine, which became known as "beard money." Some say the law was declared because the czar could not grow a beard himself.

In 1695, a window tax was raised in England on all houses that had more than six windows.

Before the 1800s, people in the United States who could not pay their debts were often thrown into debtors' prison. Many owed no more than $10.

In the Middle Ages, pepper was a highly valued spice. Many European cities became wealthy due to the importation of pepper. Taxes could be paid with it, and soldiers were often rewarded for their victories with bonuses of the spice.

In 1789, Benjamin Franklin wrote the following famous quote: "In this world, nothing can be said to be certain, except death and taxes."

In 1862, Abraham Lincoln signed the first income tax law. It required any person who made more than $800 to pay taxes. However, only 1 percent of the American people at that time made more than that.

In 1913, the entire U.S. tax code was only 16 pages long. Today, it is more than 9,000 pages.

In 1952, Albert Einstein was quoted as saying: "The hardest thing in the world to understand is income taxes."

$$X^2 - Y = \frac{(Z + X / 5)}{Y\%}$$

$$\frac{2X}{1-Z}$$

$$23 / Z < Y$$

SALARY
× 20%
= INCOME TAX

The Internal Revenue Service (IRS) loses billions of dollars every year from people who do not pay their taxes.

Denmark has the highest tax rate in the world. In return for the high taxes, citizens have free health care, free higher education, and many more benefits.

If you earn more than $400 in one year babysitting, you have to file an income tax form with the U.S. government.

The original deadline for filing tax returns in the United States was March 15. It changed to April 15 in 1954 because the tax codes had become more complicated.

Today, the chances of being audited by the IRS are less than 1 percent. However, in 1914, your chances of being audited were much higher. In fact, every single one of the 357,598 tax returns was audited that year.

# Glossary

**auction**—a sale during which items are sold to the person who offers the most money

**audit**—a review of accounts and tax returns by a trained accountant

**balance**—money left after you make a deposit or withdrawal into a money account

**banknotes**—paper money; also called bills and cash

**bankrupt**—not able to pay what is owed

**brigade**—a large group of people organized for a certain purpose

**currency**—the type of money a country uses

**debt**—something that is owed to another

**deposit**—money put into a bank account

**Great Depression**—a period in the United States in the 1930s when many businesses failed and people lost jobs

**estate**—a large piece of land

**forgers**—people who copy something in order to cheat

**fortune**—great wealth

**heiress**—a woman who is to receive money or property from a person who has died

**income**—money received for work done

**income tax**—a tax on a person's wages and other income

**inherited**—property or money one person receives after another person has died

**inscribed**—carved or written words or letters on something

**insurance**—protection against loss or damage

**loan**—money that is borrowed with a plan to pay it back

**philanthropy**—a charitable act or gift

**salary**—money paid to someone for work done

**slavery**—the practice of owning people; slaves are not free and must do what their owners tell them to do

**taxes**—money that people or businesses must give to the government to pay for what the government does

**vault**—a safe room or compartment to store things of value

**will**—a legal document that states what a person wants done with everything he or she owns after the person dies

# Index

Aesop, Jeffrey 31
Alexander, Harry 26
American Revolution 14, 15, 21
Astor, John Jacob 5
auctions 20, 22, 28

Babylonia 12, 30
bait 18
banknotes 14, 15
Bank of England 14
Bank of North America 14
bank robberies 11, 18
bankruptcy 9
banks 11, 13, 14, 15, 16, 19
barter 26
baseball cards 21
beans 26
Bettencourt, Liliane 9
billionaires 4, 9
books 11, 14, 22
bread 5, 11
Breedlove, Sarah 9

CC Camp (Candyman) 25
Carnegie, Andrew 5
cash 26
Cardback, Warren 18
check 12, 13, 14, 15
Cinderella stamps 25
coding 27
comic books 21
Cook, Frederick 22
Crassus, Marcus Licinius 5
credit cards 18
crime 11
currency 15, 26, 27, 29, 31

Debtor prison 11
Declaration of Independence 20
diamonds 25

Disney, Walt 9
dollhouses 28
Dr. Seuss 21

Einstein, Albert 21

Farmers Bank 15
fish oil 29
Federal Reserve Bank 19
Fields, W.C. 16
forgery 22
Fort Knox 19
Franklin, Benjamin 33
Fuller, Ida Mae 31

Gachet, Paul (Dr.) 23
Gates, Bill 9
Geffen, David 10
Getty, Jean Paul 5
G-Loves 22
gizzard pennies 26
gold 4, 19, 28
Great Depression 6
Green, Hetty Howland 8
gwinnett, Button 20
Gybbons, William 17

Hazel Mountain Corporation 9

insurance 31
interest 13
Internal Revenue Service (IRS) 26

Jacob, Gideon 11
Jevier, Victoria 11
Jefferson, Thomas 11, 15

Kennedy, John F. 8

labor notes 31
libraries 5, 21, 27
limestone 26
Lincoln, Abraham 30
loans 12, 13, 16, 19

Mason, Budge, 10

McCulloch, Robert, 10
millionaires, 1, 5, 6, 7, 8, 11
money crazy, 25
Model T Ford automobiles, 8
Morris, Patrick O. Stone, 13
Morgan, J.P., 5
Mott, Lewis, 25

rail, 29
Nordstrom, Over, 17

oil, 29
Over, Robert, 29

Pulitzer, 9
Trapper, 28
Prince, czar of Russia, 22
petroleum, 9, 30
philanthropy, 5, 6
Picasso, Pablo, 25
pocketbook, 16, 17
playing cards, 20

Radcliffe, Dwight, 21
Ridely, William J., 22
Rockefeller, John D., 3, 6
Rowling, J.K., 11

Sears, 19
Shakespeare, William, 7
shells, 24
shopping malls, 25
Smith, Edward, 13
Social Security, 16
stamps, 21
Stone, Patrick, 13
Stone, 29
Stone family
Stone, 29
Stone of change, 9

Lewis, 29, 30, 31
Tei, Lewis, 29
Stockholm, czar, 29
Temple, Shirley, 8
Teapot, 29

Vanderbilt, Cornelius, 5
Van Gogh, Vincent, 23

Wagner, Honus, 21
Walker, C.J., 6
Washington, George, 31
Weitzman, Steve, 23
Williams, Maurice, 22
Willis, 3, 4, 42
Windsor, Duke, 42
Woods, Tiger, 9
Wynn, Jack, 9

Young Americans Bank, 16

# To Learn More

**More Books to Read**

**On the Web**

## Look for all of the books in the Freaky Facts series:

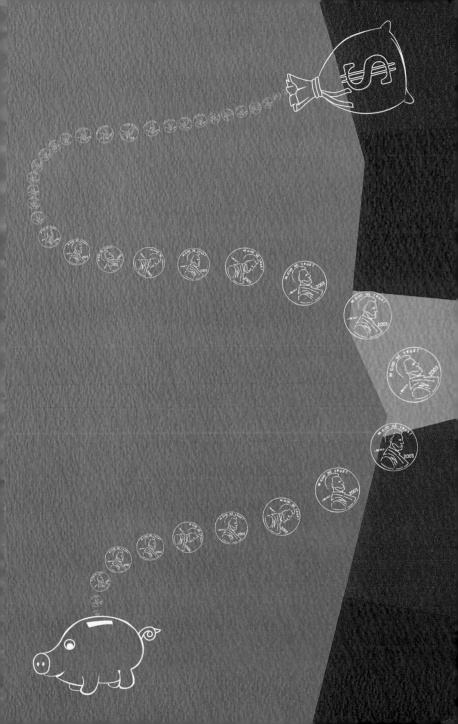